TUNALUNA

alurista

Aztlan Libre Press
San Antonio, Texas

First Edition

San Antonio, Texas 78223
210.531.9505
www.aztlanlibrepress.com
editors@aztlanlibrepress.com

Dedicated to the promotion, publication and
free expression of Xican@ Literature and Art

Publishers/Editors:
Juan Tejeda
Anisa Onofre

Veteran@s Series

alurista.
    Tunaluna: selected and new poems
    ISBN-10: 0-9844415-0-6
    ISBN-13: 978-0-9844415-0-1
    1. Chicanos-Poetry. 2. Mexican-American-Poetry.
    3. Bilingual Poetry, American. 4. Political Poetry,
    American.

Library of Congress Control Number: 2010908051

Aztlan Libre Press thanks the following individuals: Judithe Hernández for the brilliant cover of this book; Bryce Milligan, publisher of Wings Press, for his expertise and support; David Mercado Gonzales for the ALP logo and just for being a carnal; Rosemary Catácalos, Executive|Artistic Director of Gemini Ink, for her apoyo; and Angela Martínez, Paul Vaughn and Morton Neikrug for their technical guidance. Also, a very special gracias to our familias and friends for helping us realizar un sueño.

Cover Artist: Judithe Hernández's career began in the midst of the momentous decade of the 1960's. As part of the first wave of artists who formed the California Chicano art and mural movements, she is regarded as an important visual artist of the period. In 1974 she became the only female member of the legendary East Los Angeles artist collective "Los Four," which included Frank Romero, Roberto de la Rocha, Gilbert Luján, and the late Carlos Almaraz. Her professional career spans more than forty years, with exhibitions in the United States, Europe, and Mexico; including the ground-breaking first exhibition of contemporary Chicano art in Europe: *Le Demon des Anges*. Her work, which is part of many public, private, and museum collections, has been described by Dr. Chon Noriega (Chicano Studies Research Center, UCLA) as illustrating "the formation of a unique political aesthetic and Chicana/o consciousness that continues to inform her work in provocative and stunning ways."

Tunaluna is the second artistic collaboration of these two creative forces in Chicano culture. In 1971, Judithe Hernández illustrated alurista's first volume of poetry: *Floricanto en Aztlán*.

Cover Art: *Las Musas del Desierto* (detail) © Judithe Hernández

For more information about Judithe Hernández, please visit her website: www.jhnartestudio.com

Back cover photo by Christopher Gardner; courtesy Metro Newspapers Silicon Valley

Aztlan Libre Press logo by David Mercado Gonzales

Two thousand copies of this first edition of *Tunaluna* by alurista were printed on 55 pound Edwards Brothers Natural Paper containing a high percentage of recycled fiber. Titles were set in Nueva Std type style, the text in Adobe Caslon Pro.

Mesa de Contentos

Introduction

I first met alurista in 1975 at the University of Texas in Austin. He was a Visiting Lecturer there for a couple of years teaching courses and already a legendary loco en la Literatura Xicana. I was a junior at the university and involved en el Movimiento Chicano with various organizations at the school and in the community including MAYO (Mexican American Youth Organization) and the Raza Unida Party when I enrolled in one of his Chicano Poetry classes. This course proved to be a turning point that greatly influenced the direction of my life and my life's work. It was through alurista and this class of estudiantes and emerging escritores y poetas que se me prendió el foco. Everything came together, full circle, so to say, much like it has come together again today, and it was the new beginning of my American Indian spirituality and Xicano cultural identity. It was the new beginning of my work with poesía, música, danza Azteca, education, Chicano arts organizations and arts administration. It was the beginning of my work with Literatura Xicana and publications and independent Chicano publishing. In a very real sense, it was the beginning of Aztlan Libre Press, 35 years later, mas o menos, with the publication of this book, *Tunaluna*, our first and alurista's tenth collection of poetry.

But it all began in alurista's Chicano Poetry class at U.T. Austin where we met once a week, first on campus, then off campus, then at alurista's home, or one of the other writer's homes. We read our poetry, short stories, locuras, discussed, critiqued, talked politics, got organized, made música, marchamos, leímos en la universidad, la comunidad, and at the end of this course we published *Trece Aliens*, a compilation of writings and drawings from twelve students and alurista. I only have one copy in my files, copyrighted 1976 by the authors. An 8 ½" x 11" spiral bound, xeroxed copied, black on white bond paper with black on blue slightly thicker cover stock and a Cecilio García-Camarillo black ink drawing on the cover entitled "Un bato con las manos abiertas" whose two outspread hands are drawn with the letters that spell "silencio" and whose black-hatted face is composed of words that read "para mi raza tortillas cósmicas" with a cucaracho coming out of the bottom of the drawing. I think we added that cucaracho to Cecilio's drawing. Con permiso, carnal. It was my first publication. I remember collating the pages by hand assembly-style, and at the end of the short introduction to *Trece Aliens* alurista wrote: "la temática de la obra es el resultado de diálogos abiertos en los cuales exploramos la alienación humana – particularmente xicana – y sus causas. la dedicamos a todos los 'aliens' como nosotros, con esperanzas de que el dia llegue cuando las fronteras no existan."

Thus began a journey that would immerse me in the Chicano Cultural Renaissance and working with many projects and organizations including the Conjunto Aztlan, LUChA (League of United Chicano Artists), the Festival Estudiantil Chicano de Arte y Literatura, Capitán-General Andrés Segura and Xinachtli, the Guadalupe Cultural Arts Center, Palo Alto College, and others.

All along this journey I have been involved with writing and publishing in one way or another. In 2008, my compañera, Anisa Onofre (who is also a poet/writer and currently the Director of the Writers in Communities Program at Gemini Ink here in San Antonio), and I decided to fulfill a dream and create an independent Chicano publishing company dedicated to the promotion of Xican@ Literature and Art. In 2009 Aztlan Libre Press began to become a reality. In the spirit of Cecilio Garcia-Camarillo and *Caracol*, plans are underway to publish *Nahualliandoing Dos*, a chapbook of collected poemas and writings in three languages, Nahuatl, Español and English, and a coloring book for children. *Tunaluna* is the first publication in a Veteran@s Series, and we're also making plans for a Nuevas Voces Series and an Aztlan Libre Press Premio en la Literatura Xicana, among other projects. It's a labor of love, pero como preguntó la camarada, "is there any other kind?"

This book just kinda fell into our proverbial, as they say, laps. I hadn't talked to maestro alurista in years and Nisa found his website one evening. We e-mailed him and his son, Zamná, responded with a telephone number for him in Tijuana. I called him that night and we talked and caught up a bit on our San Anto-Tijuana telefonazo and when I mentioned Aztlan Libre Press just starting up, he said he had a latest manuscript of poemas he was going to send us. To our surprise, a couple of weeks later we received a typed manuscript for *Tunaluna* via snail-mail. We read the manuscript and were amazed and maybe just laughing un poquito that Aztlan Libre Press, a just-started-never-published-nada-small-Chicano-press-con-poca-feria, might publish alurista's tenth book of poems. So I called alurista again a little later in the week and presented the idea to him and de volada he said "simón k yes," and sas, just like that, after months of trabajo and editing and decisions, "aquí estamos y no nos vamos."

Another interesting convergence was with Judithe Hernández. She contacted us after seeing one of our internet postings about alurista's book. Judithe had done the illustrations and artwork for alurista's first book, *Floricanto en Aztlán*, in 1971. She offered her beautiful cover artwork and design for *Tunaluna* as a gift to alurista. Another connection had come full circle.

alurista is without a doubt one of the seminal and most influential voices in the history of Chicano Literature. A pioneering poeta del Movimiento Chicano of the 60s and 70s, he broke down barriers in the publishing world with his use of multilingual and interlingual writings in three or more languages including English, Español and Nahuatl. But he is more than that: a maestro and mentor, camarada y duende destrampado, padre, abuelo, Ph.D profe and publisher. Some have called him the Poet Laureate of Aztlán, and he's defintely one of them because he has been one of the most important poetic voices of the people, del Pueblo Chicano. He's a thinker and philosopher, an organizer and activist. He was instrumental in developing Chicano Studies in the U.S. and a co-founder of MEChA (Movimiento Estudiantil Chicano de Aztlán). He also founded the Festival de Flor y Canto, the first national festival dedicated to Chicano literature and art. His writings were key to reclaiming our history, heritage and MeXicano cultural identity. Author of "El Plan Espiritual de Aztlán," he integrated American Indian language, symbols, spirituality and the concept of Aztlan as the Chicano Nation into our literature which reconnected us to our raíces, our birth right, our ties to this land, and in turn, to the cosmic consciousness.

alurista's poetry can be cryptic and encoded at times, considered to be beyond the reach of the common working man and woman del pueblo. While this crítica is true to a certain extent (isn't this true of all poetas?), he has always written for the people and is very conscious of the colonized status of Chicanos within the U.S. and how the poor, working class people have been exploited economically by this Capitalist system and its attendant educational institutions that have been motivated by the greed of the rich and the profit principle. It was this historical, cultural, social, economic and political understanding that led him to the realization of a revolutionary aesthetic that stressed the importance of art and literature as a transforming tool and cultural weapon in the struggle for social justice.

Con mucho respeto y honor, Aztlan Libre Press is proud to present to you *Tunaluna*, alurista's décima, and our inaugural publicación. This collection of 52 poemas and writings is classic alurista: passionate, sensuous and political. He takes us on a time trip through the first decade of the 21st Century where he bears witness to the "Dubya" wars, terrorism, oil and $4 gallons of gas, slavery, and ultimately, spiritual salvation and transformation through his connection to the Creator, and the Lord 'n' Lady of the Dawn, and Buddha, and flores y cantos. The "Word Wizard of Aztlan" is at his razor-sharp best, playing with his palabras as well as with our senses and sensibilities. He is the tlamantinime, keeper of the black and red ink who gives the people a face and heart. He is the tlatoani, who speaks for the people. He conjures up César Chávez and Corky González, maize and salsa con chile, pyramids and suns, urakán serpents and águilas in flight, then descends into the depths of the underworld and "labyrinths of this neofascist burrocracia" where workers sweat, bleed, and die, only to be resurrected again in "...cosmic love and spiritual freedom...yes. love. be we."

alurista is a Xicano poet for the ages and a chronicler of la Nueva Raza Cózmica. With *Tunaluna* he trumpets the return of Quetzalcoatl, the feathered-serpent of Aztec and Mayan prophecy, and helps to lead us out of war and into the dawn of a new consciousness and sun, el Sexto Sol, nahuicoatl, cuatro serpiente, sun of justice.

In tlanextia in tonatiuh
Que su sol sea brillante
May your sun be brilliant

Juan Tejeda

Dedicatoria

A mi madre, hermana Nelly, hermanos y sobrina/os. 2 my godchildren especialmente Maosorio.

A mis mentores Juan Gómez-Quiñones, Gary Keller, Carlos Blanco and Karen Van Hooft.

2 my children: Tizoc, Maoxiim, Zamná & Zahi and all those who they love and respect.

2 my grandchildren: Abigaixiim, Andrés and Damaris Esteli.

To all my relations & partners in crime 'specially Ocelotl.

in tlanextia, in tonatiuh

IN TLOKE, IN NAHUAKE

y pórtense bien!

y si nó...invítenme...sin vergüenza

¡sinvergüenzas!

Prólogo al Decálogo

This, my tenth collection of poetry will be published in 2010: "la quinta ola"...the previous waves being 1965-1974 when RACE was the principal contradiction in Xicano writing and U.S.A. consciousness. 1975-1984 when CULTURAL contradictions became central to Xicano ideology realizing that Mexican by definition includes Amerindian, African, European and Asian cultures 'n' races though clearly dominated by Judaeo-Christian, Anglo-Saxon, machista transnational cultural imperialism. The third wave, 1985-1994, then focused on GENDER, when most Xicana writers bloomed most assertively and right on target 'n' time. During 1995-2004, the CLASS contradiction predictably became the focus of our literary production either by including class discourse or by omitting it, it was there and most important. We now come to the fifth ola which encompasses ALL contradictions, 2005-2014. Clearly, the end of the Piscean Era and the beginning of the Aquarian Age: leaving faith and devotion for reason and wisdom; the return of Quetzalcoatl, December 21, 2012...according to Mayan chronology and prophecy. 2 b certain today.

> As once said before:
> "what it is
> be what it does
> could never b
> what it was
> nor could it b
> what it will b
> what it'll come
> 2 pass shall b
> when what does
> b what it is"
>
> ...arroz!!!

do enjoy y compartan la colección *Tunaluna*
Los Trece Aliens live forth
in this here mi décima

Luna

lunatuna
fluttering
below belly
pasiones swooping
down deep
gathering storms
treasuring
rainergías pacíficas
marítimas, montañescas
abotona tu vientre, maja
easles b ready
to capture flight
entre tus aguas claras
allow flow
...reflect...
clama la milpa
eye your center
cherish thigh
hug torso
b one
with duende within
discover
sun risa raza roja

Secuelan

secuelan, las nubes dan sombra

       ya no se trata de balas escuelas

    no siguen, no valen los tiros

      ni tampoco los machetes

    a menosque abran brecha

        vereda esta selvavaricia

que solo busca, quiere, indaga

    where is the gold? glory?

          god?

    even today lo encuentran presto

    prieto, prietóleo y negro diamante tanque

      twenty karats now in yellow

    pink, b white...even.....black

         match naught sweat

       in the oil fields o' cemanahuacarabia

         no se escuelan, invierten

se posesionanapropiando

         eurogringos bankean

consin korán, torahean

       con biblia en kuwait

tapas negando las asoleadas tardes

      del pueblo espadeando

      las espinacas

      las lechugas chinas

solo existen en sus mesas frescas

    ...si hay diablo...no 'ta en el infierno, sabes

entre nosotros!...labra!

   existescucha

Birdnests

birdnests off the balcony

                                        gather comrades

      off the road books b read

'n' words b written

                    orders given

         click thy boots

               we b here

                                  'n' there

    'n' our peoples shall b fed

               we

       remain

             standing

with our slingshots in our hands

no goliath will prevail

Rest

rest b

full

alert

affirmation

love

acceptance

see

observe

ask

release

acquire naught

negate naught the present u

comparing thee to an idea of

perfection

perfection is not being

being b in a state of becoming

meaning not that all being is a state

becoming

perfect

rather

a state of becoming more itself

dare let go

denial fear and defiance go

recognize that quality equals

consciousness of object and

subject

in affirmation love and acceptance

trust the miracle of self

Man

man in jungle
seven days calling
                    out quetzal
            out snake
        guarding flank for
                    jaguar
            self sacrifice
        for others in light
            darkness 'n' ignorance
                    2 b warded off
                        quetzal plumes
                                        one snake
                            kill fear
            courage abounds
                    flute 'n' drum
                    tambor breathe
                            'n'
            roars volcanes
                            pouring lavamagma
                the earth cleanses
                            herself
                                    our mother
                                    our father
                            spiral
                    as all do on earth
            'n' thee
                            material universe
the owl hoots wisdom

enemies
of life
liberté
compassion para todos
en nuestro sistema solar
Chac........Tláloc
now weeps 4 all of us
corn sprouts
LA TORTILLA <u>ES</u>
PARA TODOS
one man
one woman
4
legs

4

eyes
4
ears
two tongues
kissing
4
cheeks

4

hands
4
nostrils

4

brows
two ovaries
two testicles
two oracles
2 b 1

Convencido

convencido estoy
        que todo poeta
    debe ser exterminado
ninguna república
      los tolera
casi como a congo, o tongo lele
    mau, mau
        la hora llega, la la
como la lluvia
       temprana
          ...cállate!
      simonto lo meo
era una santidad
       ...qué nó?
sino...pos kkk, la tuya!
las cruces y los venenos abundan
rehusemos entonces las azúcares
     que nos ofrece el imperio

la sal sudor de nuestro pueblo acribilla cualquier bob osada

Tee Roar

merriam a state of words

      intense fright isms

bushisms...not buddhism?

                   state terrorism?...

      tolstoy...war...peace

           sí, vea ría...siberia?!!!

      rak i put thee

           eight ball in

                the left ran

           corner pocket

                withdraw

your money 'n' your guns

           'tis b eight...ball

u loose bush!...play gulf!?

           like granpa did

           Mexican golfopétreo?

              we survive!

      state?...occupy a nation?

own...ass... a tenant?

      vit all your shoulders

             state te roar ism...

...u ever heard 'bout that

                  ...georgie???

                  ...junior???

chain in 'n' out

      off Cuba

      Irak...Irán...Siria...Afghanistán

keep thy bombs to your ranch

      learn to ride arabian horses

hoses...water?

thy lawns?

golf courses?

grass?

while people thirst on earth
with piano
...teclas...zonzótez!
...cenotes?
throw thy jewels
down!!!
we don't need your bombs
ride a stallion!!!
u b thrown off
thy b ass
it were? barf!!!
drink powdered milk...regurgit
ate pen...déjote!!!
canto y bailo
nuestra sonrisa
y ké!
aquí estamos
y no nos vamos!

Urakán

urakán serpent
    otra vez, rambles
        tremors the earth
            roaring still
    otra vez, trembles
there b no barking left
    in this here rain
gutters abound under
    homeless warriors
ignite their hearts
    peace remains
        within
            in with out
know no nothing being
    blooming
        being one with all
own no nothing seeing
    swimming
    singing song with all
so there b tabaco
so there b hops
so there b fuego
so there b ice
let then b lava
    that is all that is
...rain...thunder...
ura kán in Tlalticpac

On My Head

on my head standing

>   pointing upwards treasuring

tu presencia mujercita adorándote

>   ahora como siempre única tú eres

todos los seres imaginables

>   i sit before u

i am holy happy

>   when i pillage 'n' plunder

>   roses off a Bush

>   that world rather

>   spurt petróleo

>   steal votes 'n' b

white house dweller ass florida

>   towers

b gone aware b of the scent

>   a flower produces

...thy cannot, will

>   not consume

the black gold

>   off the working classes sweat!

Gazing

gazing, grazing en el tren, tranvía, ni que fuera villa
zapata...tal vez, with leather white tennis shoes
                                    la raza rifa los files
rifles
            las nubes ya se acumulan
                            si tu quieres estos lagos
tendrás tú que ser la garza
                        estos árboles y estepas mariposean
            eucaliptos con sus postes de teléfono
y los cerros bien acordes hacen melodías en rieles
                                sin recoger una uva
                                    y los files y los fieles
                se acoplan al chaparral
y la raza lázara! lázara! lázara!
                                            nos dice
                levántate!
            papaloteando llaves ante los truenos
                            relámpagos que presagían
huraaacanados movimientos telúricos
                            volcanes derramando magma
                                healing itself motherearth
lluvias devastadoras
                            labios que brotan en sonrisa
plena
ese calor que emana de tu cuerpo
tide us over another wave

Son

son las cinco
      en punto
            de la mañana
    no hay
    toro
        que matar
    ni torah que recordar
          hay enanos con sombras
  que opacan a cualquiera
             con sus balas
             con sus matracas
   hay enanos
      que ni
          conocen el campo
    en que nace el rocío
          que da alas al korán
y nos dicen que la biblia salvatodos
        a las cinco en punto de la
 ¿tarde?
    es ella la única
          regla
      yacecielo
 ayam

Cae

la luz cae, el sol se aparece, presencia...brisa
fluye!
va'l pueblo
flechas obsidianas.......ojos
te dá pena?

enpeñate! tus piernas rueda
ojo te redima

atrapa atención hoy
jardines en el desierto de los cantos
bruma de nuestro   oleaje
aquí!   los papagallos tumbalean
congas

con violines eléctricos
..... dios nos libre!
vela mecha pólvora

now what?

canto solar...lunar

marea
y la ola rifa

tableando espuma
sin azotar las rocas

llueve
ta'deo...dos...dios...os
vos tu él, ella?

quo vadis?
.......os acompaño!

veredea
flechea nopal.....águila

Brake

brake earth en mil pedacitos
learn to row
palm 'n' elm give us shade
learn to net 'n' eat fish
mercury, black gold...not needed
nor desired
how many feathers
must a bald eagle bear
before we stop the carnage
...mil pedacitos...
mil pedacitos...pa'que broten
volcanes!
.....que tiemble la tierra
ser ó no self
shelf that thought coming
let it go
allow the rowing 2
take us 2 la
playa
a chore
b 4 us!
pyramids re main
sol id
we re member
play
ego lay dead
'n'
sub
conscious
tell 'bout the mil
pedacitos
en los
o sé años

Bona

bona note... good note... bona sera...good morning

night?...... departure... otra vés?

why me i ask?.....'tis travel

makesme entero

pero, pero...kí!....

no hay perros

puros gatos somos todos

servidores

want thy

mint julep?

master...mistress?...mint

b right a long...casi did

could produce such

service

what it b

b tonto ranger lone

cybernetic transnational

slavery kimo

sabee net inter

none of us will bear

any chains

bona note camp es ina

no more grapes to pick

b there contract!?   ...sign it!..... 'tis b

our unión

sin vergüenza

...por favor! ... aquí...firma!

somos uno!

este   amanecer   STRIKE!!!!!

We're

we're the fool blooded indians
frontal lobotomy
rather than bottled coors
in front o'me... tu sabe'
adonde apunte el huarache...vamo'
i fly 'n' hover...joya
gema de mi vida
below your belly button
esmeralda de mi alma
let us relish
the buttons of our pasión
paz i on
paz ion
pasión
paz si...on...adelante!

Nani

nani buena fué

        nani buena é

    única de'pué

mis sueños .....dijo...son

     hijo...pa'los que quieren ser

hacer...conocer...y ser más

        otra vez lo que ya

son

      así, así aprender a ver,

  a cocer jolitos i rosito

    'prender a ser 'tillas

con salsa buena ...come

con ganas sudor

con alma placer

       hay que

  estudiar

simón que yes

   ¡clarín que sí!

Cerciorémosnos

cerciórate...que'l aplauso no sea
    ni pa'l pastor ni pa' la moneda
      centurión..... soldado
        cent tu rión, sentaos, come
piña, mamey..... y zapote
        pa' los pobres
transpiremos por los poros
porque en anglosangronía
            no yace ni el coro
ní en zapatour
      ní en el camote dulce
           anunciado
    con   ruedas cantos
            más allá
    de sus chiflidos
        pripendejadas
      ¡cerciorémosnos!

A X

a xingar, plantar

seresmero

buena semilla, tranquilos

a smile energyabrazo, planta, camina

piensa, obra, se xin zaz

zen

zazen

xa

x

en

e

wu   tai

4 mi

leía, lía, leí

leo

sit lo'

pa'florecer

en verbo

xing...xinaxtli...!

Ina

sí, tú sabes, camino cuatro guerrillas
la quinta, me la mataron tuyo i ke soy
solonosotros pos que decimos, nos faltan
tortillas
palimentar a este pueblo continente
que quieres que haga...ajos limones ojos
yo que sé divina
esta página, mejor córtala
tal vez, ves el amor que nos no, no pos sí
nos sí pos sí, motiva, nó?
tu eres ella...dios
uno yo .....una tú
vos i yo semossemas simas somos
sumos, sabes que sí
yo no se mentir prendolavela para ver un poquito de
luz
abandona las cadenas
no sacrifiques   la hiedra
que la yerba muera!
amorosamente alegra tu corazón, tu divinidad
sé ..... tú, única
un dia...una luna...un hombre
con túnica
que pisa su propio rostro
para iluminar el tuyo
soñará contigo
a'nque los yankis quieran robarte
has de permanecer   jitamao
crece, merece, sé
como tú ere' karen

Go

go girl, go girl, go girl
    let the vacas locas blancas bilingües
      displace all our sisters
        under the guise
      off...'firmative action
      'fter all
"...we b minorities too!
      ...u know what i'm saying
white daddy?"
      do say
          hola!
        to the mexican
    babysitter
        i mean the xicana
caring for, four?
      of your güerito children?
go girl
    go girl
        go girl
            go girl
aquí no hay
      hombres
        y los duendes?
           solo en flor
how's your spinach carnalita?

Si Acaso

si acaso la talla importa
no tengo mil leguas
botas
a'nque sea yo felino
bendígate a tí la estampa
nos ilumina
gozemos la luz ternura
que'n la risa es vitamina
aquí nadie se apresura
pero
tu hermosura
tu sonrisa pura
brilla
sé tú inteligente
deja'trá'
to'amargura
álguien
te pinta....
.....frescura

Take Over

take over
        lanza al vate
   a los
      tlacuilos
coronados
   con destino
          murales cariños
      en las paredes que brincas
con pigmentos
            comunales
la raza
   así
      reconstruye
su calaca
     corazón
        cabeza
   y
      celebra
    nuestralegría

I Rak

i ran, ó me¡

while libélulas

frolic

along hummingbirds

libating honey

Pluck

pluck thy own

    mine b based

       a'ready

flowering

       well seeded

'tis people

'tis class

     'tis race to thee

finish thy debt

          pay up!......íjole!

   ...y pos qué?...a pus qué?

apoco hay frijoles y tortillas

     para

      todos?...arroz?!

¿cultivamos nosotros chile, calabazas...tabaco?

   lo que nos puede alimentar

       mandar oraciones a nuestro señor

   y señora

     a maize ¿in g minor

we do, ke nó?.....amasamos

     please do not disturb

u may find thyself surrendered by

   guerreras

      mexicanindias

Wanabee

u wanabee a b?

b wasp?

pepenar flores

ampollas...veneno

b your self

b?...what?

u wanna b?

entonces, sé!

do sting if thy must.....hurt

some

bodi else

none of us can or will tolerate

in califaztlán, coloradaztlán, y menos en texaztlán

essa, esse date cuenta

wanabee

que'l camino se tiene que andar

sin poisons

sin inflammations

con toda tu piel y tus huesos

tus sesos

tus besos

do learn to love

u! first!

the other 'n' the otters will

shall

gather clams 'n' crack them on thy belly

arizonaztlán

nuevo

méxico

pearl

Hablando

hablando de palabras
        "póbrecito"
nunca me ha gustado
        the word simply flees
with a diminutive
        that avoids class y complejos
militarindustrialistas
        arabíndio... "póbrecito"
b what bankerobberbaron say
        "thy house b
repossessed 'n' occupied"
        "póbrecita" mozárabe
b term used
claiming "thy" body
        at a morgue
"póbrecito" es la palabra
        que disculpa'l estado terrorista
a todos los que producen
        LA POBREZA
de los que les sirven y rodean
        así pues, no maldigo, ni digo "póbrecito"
b he/she que se sienta sobre sus manos
procreandomuerte y masacres inauditas
        necesidad, ignorancia y miedo
sin labrar el verbo que florece
        en libertamorinteligentespiritúnico

We're

we're
    donde las plumas abundan
donde, duende
    apunta huarache
la XIA...Xicano Intelligence Agency
    my loft es tu cantón   .
canta further
    génesis
    anyway
cualquier ox?
    whatever...siempre
alguien

É

él   tranquilo

  ella   la mora

   amora

    amor él danza

  que se yergue inpune

    ver sin miedo

él, que atesora flor...ella

    y canta su corazón

   volando con sus manos vé

huaraches dedos, ella?

   descalzo él?

     ...quién?

  sin zapatos?

   platillo volador

 a tre vete Mexicano...

   ¡volvemos! sabés?!

si nos corres...no hay tenichoose

 ...porque, sabes?

   esta flor

    dá uvas

  este camino

   cantaciego

   es ver mío

     y

  tuyo es el baile

   anda lucía

What Now... Corn

what now dog, bush barking hot
    pos orale pues gato 'n' howl hoot
      lo que es, olive, busca
it b. yes! it b oil, black gold!
              petroleum
      what it b about...a boot?
zorri for all of them flying, falling
            metal birds...
      no, really the aeroplanos
         the bombs 'r' now directed
    at rak 'n' ran... or the ganis...why I ask?
the answer b clear...money 'n' oil pumps
       ¿cuál es tu santa verdad, jorgito?
         nosotros nos damos cuenta
    de las tarugadas
           que ya has cometido
           Senior
señor?   ...que gran explotador!
the earth disagrees with u, your family
          'n' your economic plans
$$4$$
        let alone the estamos undidos
de angloamérica.....perdonen la palabra...pendejo...
      get a clue 'n' balance
        our budget...baboso
quit beating 'round' your own   ..mr pres
       act like one for all
     else there b none ....zonzo
cats abound midst gringolandia

No Hay

no hay canto
no hay rosa
que iguale
tu mellow día
armonía
de
...cuán capaces
somos!
los milagros
gracias
bomba...!
ayer pasé x tu casa
y me
ladra
ron
los libros
...quise'garrar
una letra
y me'mbarre
todas las plumas
.....a volar se ha dicho!

Goating

goating...gloating
their own evil web
reeking
greed without aim wander
capturing alacranes
spelling
their own demise
while libélulas frolic
along hummingbirds
libating   miel
trampolines de tragedia lanzando

designs for a new world

con ganas, coño
eres lo que eres
sé tú gracia
porque las gracias te adornan
somos   capaces
estudia...enseña

lo que somos

Sol

solo u chon con ó sin
compromisos...de cuero mija
maja
paja no mereces
algodón tampoco
ni tampico
change your pant aletas sola
des
pués
te darás cuerda
de quien ploquea y josemartinea
...y te llamas cubana?
u india...reservada
...pa' quién?
tierra!!!...ash 2 ash
si llamas y amas y ya más
ye flat i major
tú perdida...yo en el llano
encontrado   no contigo...conmigo
evítame ante todo perón
men ti rosa piano thyself down
the stairs of your self importance...let go
blood flowing everywhere
...profesa tu tecla y vívela
...'jita!!!

Mesas

mesas para dox
    xicas...pero yo que sé
solo tinta i no soy pulpo
    a'nque me corten los tentáculos
      abrazo a todo mi pueblo
sin tentar willow weeps naught
    when the tronco been cut
to branches euskadia, xiapas, nicaragua
    cuba ya...
irlanda...what up with english only!!!?
    que caiga la mierda sobre los y las
      que la cagan 'garra
spoon 'n' pluck thyself from depths
    of self mexican denial
that u have yet to tinkerbell
    met or will meet ball foot
    all on the green prevails
stomping grounds that long a go, go?
    cajas
    were disco!!!...today
      congas...mágicas manos
otra vez sonrisas, pan peter
    .....why not?

Quet

zal
yo llamo al
pequeño ocelote
rugir de plumas
...tigrillo
maize...maize
te quiero ave santa
canta...vale
enséñame vereda ....cañón
que yo sé que sé
caminar, el andar, zi
sereno, pleno
de luna, playa y arena
hay olas
traigo luz
moro...
maya...
gitano ... lindamor mexica
imploro, apéate chula
el cuero que nos rodea
toca tambores, y flautas
fuman tonales

Vale

vale

                             mago sin capa

        escapa de cualquier telar

       spider también hormiga

       conozco a los alacranes

           alá cranes

              con cola

     pero que te cuento toro

           si tu tenéis ya tus cuernos

cabra

              león con melena

          no me importa elena

           ni su caballo de troya

        ni lo que venció a aquiles

              viva

           un puño campesino

           que atesora lechugas

    fresas y uvas

          con el pueblo de emiliano

XICANO

         no soy bonaparte

            pero de los buenos

      zapatistas

Pa' César y Corky

what for the rush and bloody pain
what for the blooming and the rain
what for the quest and odyssey
what for the swimming and the sea, see
there b no shore or beach that anyone
can reach
and breathe, inhale, exhale, and love
all seems to ooze the stress that greed has carved in us
surely our species should be meek
before our motherearth's volcanoes
storms and huracanes
tornadoes, floods and tremors
and there we b secreting poisons for all leggeds, wingeds,
fish and even trees

what for the rush and bloody pain
we'll surely die, but then

we dig deeper in our heartmindspiritbody
and nurture glow and warmth
and light and peace and patience
and gladness and gardens
and gather all in oneness
and end the pain and bloody rush
desiring naught
expecting naught
missing naught
simply being being

we truly have no choice...though

we imagine, dream, hope, want
 being all that we are we are all that is
 and that is all there b

césar and corky
   this b my writ to chávez y gonzález
 carnales de las sonrisas grandes
   de las carcajadas llenas
  de murales
  de cuadros, ensayos
  matadors de pendejadas
  terminators of guandajos and juanabees
   hermanos, jefes
 your "death" is but our "birth"
  porque amasteis
   entregasteis
 y hoy, como siempre,
  sois imprescindibles

En Tú

en tu casa yacen flores
cojo luz
aunque hierve jade
hacia la miel
sangre fuego somos
ardiente felicidad
sensible sol contigo
dulce momento
rosa cristalina
hermosa
sobre un solo
om bli go
turquesa
la nuestra gema flama
llama sí
nos llama
nos canta fuego
amatista

Ink

ink naught blood u b not willing to spill
think not rope u b not willing to tie
sink nut crack u b not willing to dump
fink not people u b not willing to kill
                    ink
                    think
                                        sink
                        fink
        blood
            rope
                crack people
    spill
            tie
                dump
                i
    ...no te creas!
                créate
    sé tú
            goza
                los cantos son nuestros
                    los rostros también
            ...que esperas?
                ...ama...lucha...vence!

Climbing

climbing up, thee...pyramid

i saw...u father...mother...

sun   earth

moon, grandmother

'n' thy holy gusto, maize

máscaras...con pescados!

chuy!!!

yo no soy dimes ni pesetas

gestas, soy oz elote

tú, marchanta!

vendes   cultura, ahuacates?

regresamos...ya llegué

y tú eres...adorable

cuando nos cansemos

de el   perfilamiento

y la detención policiaca

they will eat dung

in thy backyard find your weapons!

mass destruction!

gather them with thy bush burning

your own grass 'n' people will eat

kitsch...without bombs!

buttons

...don't press

Xao Lin

u spy our air
     u dare above our land
u regret the day that your plane
     hovers y aterriza bien
let no one pilot die
     camouflage   oily smirk
...el petróleo no es tuyo!
a'nque tengas muchos carros
     thee, thy, we
the Chinese have 'n' will live
     without U...S..A.
...el petróleo no es tuyo!
     ...sabes?
     ...conoces a los dinosaurios?
     pos
     aquí
we have encountered
     people
pregúntale a
     Mao
we catch u whole yankee
     do not bother
our space
     ...respect!!!
     ...trim thy bushit

Class Sweat

g. bush junior

would rather starve the children

at home and else...where?

spurt blood petróleo

steal votes

make up countries

white house dwellers

aware of the scent...of squalor

that produces naught

while merikans consume thee, Kwait, Canadalaska

sweat 'n' b happy

don't worry

habla con la gente

no more mentiras, please!

4 please...?

Simón K Yes!

you're 'n' indian
       'n' i'm not?
              nut, naught, knot?
... so b it
          my feathers
             write redblack
nowadays....daze?
                 write
'n' write 'n' write 'n' write
        some mo'
...what lawn...white house?
...what four? or five?
    who b what?
'n' who b who?
    in all honesty
i know nothing!
       ZERO
gracias a DIOS: LORD 'n' LADY
of OUR DAWN
    ...OUR DAWN?
whose is it anyway?
    ...just the thirteen jaguar bones...!

Menguante

un cuarto lunar

     menguante

  ilumina la oscura falda de la noche

barking ardillas defend their cones

   mayates crawl about endlessly

moths sink below the flame

   candles flutter over pechos

blood flows down muslos

   without pause

without truce chicharras sing

   trees b cut 'n' paper pressed

clouds settle on the range

   ...relampagea y truena

no rain to temper our drought

   cenote...papalote

ó pantano time...papá elote!

   b there any space venado

for peace, please

   regemos a nuestro ser

that it, self, may

   in deed, fact

bloom 'n' once more

     b

Distance

distance from here to there
        is equivalent to the distance
from there to here
        i can go there
u can come here
        i can come here, u can go there
from pain to love
        or fear to joy
from dark to light
        or warmth to cold
from north to south
        or east to west
from here to there
        or there to here
distance weaves unholy blankets
        closeness weaves cariño pillows
birds sing everywhere always
        songs b heard by those who listen
and dance the tune with heart
          silence prevails
arguments bear no melody
        here b no rhythm, there b no rhyme
love 'n' dare to b
          or b naught

Candela

candela
    con su llama lúcida
joytears water gardens
    entre hojas yacemos, within
nos erguimos ahuehuetes
    escuchamos la otredad, in lak ech
que nos aqueja, moramor
    y no hay cerros, mountains red
sierras aún que detengan
    nuestra tinta
la que escribe así recibe
    su corazón entregado path
dado, rendido a tus pies
    morena
        et ta zihua

Acaricio

acaricio tus cabellos
    en mis sueños
pluma dejo 'garro lápiz
    tiza pizarrón
        escribo, pinto
           claro
             dígome a mi mismo
sin cera sin mente plasma
    tu alma...me repito
sé tú todo   sol
descubre tu velo, sin máscara...sé
    re vélate...late!
vueláguilas nubes
    que te añoran, llueve, moja...maja
complace a tu tierra
    brisagua brilla
date cuentalacránméxico
    que uno somos
dos dios deo teo tao da o
    a u m ke! au...mmm
bello es tu vello
        bóveda de cenote profundo
marítimo canto
    amable sabroso sensual
vientre...sin remordimiento
era ayer...hoy tu ritmo gozo
        era'yer que tenía prisa
    hoy tranquilo así me acerco más
        a tí...razamia
        a'nque suene posesivo

razamia quiero dejarme querer
                querer dejarme y quererte
era'yer que tenía prisa
                hoy tranquilo te atesoro
                        en mi dar
                                tu paladar
hoy no apresuro el encuentro
                mas empiezo a saborear
el chispeo en tus labios
                que tú estás yá
por venir, llegar, llover
                dulcemente
derramando toda muerte
                así brotando con jugos
nueva vida bañándome'n tu luz
milagro merengue melodía sabrosa
                era'yer que tenía prisa
hoy tu cadencia, hoy tranquilo
                así os gozo
y más...y más...y más...y más
                me acoplo a tí
                        raza

S. Wart

nigger butch

chain in 'n' out

"git...a license migrant"

no la'aces not u or your burning bushit

ni aquí ni en Cuba,

ni en afghanistán

irak ó i rán...

keep thy bombs to your ranch in texas

austentatious ass, u b

learn to ride horses

Mexican style

hoses?...water

thy lawns?

throw thy jewels down!!!

we don't need any

ride a stallion!!!

b thrown off

ass it were?

eat powdered milk...

vomita!!!   bush!!!

canta y baila én y con México

the terminator

is done jr press

jorgie arbusto

quemadobscuro

Si Así Están

si así están los rieles en nocholo city como estará la estación
digo porque a veces un boleto por favor para malibú pelicans
pica mas que un pez in empire bitch and the sand is fraught
con petróleo y el oro negro en cholo vista no rifa ni retrofit
como contar las lineas de una camisa cuando en realidad es
lisa y blanca corbateando a cualquier mono que aunque en
seda se vista chango gringo queda sin pasaje to the otter
land of chumash shamans despertando platanares en lugares
conocidos como pélamela y comete la cáscara no entendieron
in the missions nevermind the franciscanos that brought
to bear a god their ancestors crucified to stain the village
with his blood como están los rieles en la santa fe si los
chinos cholean vigas y se van pa' califas there be tram rams
and buffaloes steal roaming now in kunfu spinach with a
little olive oil floating rafters down the colorado river to
the vineyards and the valleys in califas mas guitarras mas
gitanos mas taconeo mas botas mas caballos u r a peon i am
mexican 'n' she chinese y danzante la salsa con chile serrano
y sobre todo piso! la danza de la lengua que en realidad se
comunica dice la danza chale con el retrotax que la plata
abunde pa'la educación de todos pos aquí estamos y no nos
vamos graduación la tuya porque la mía 'taba floreada de
conocimientos claros ahora ni siquiera saben donde yace el
lugar donde se reunen los caballeros águilas ni hablar de los
jaguares pues le sacan al rugido y a las garras se les acabaron
las ganas y ni siquiera saben quien cual sor era juana inés ya
no hablemos de ninguna cruz ó biblioteca anathema to the
waves wallowing tiburones y no hay ceviche pa'todos solo

pa' los que mastican mierda servida pa'los que recogen la

uva que pisada beben hasta meter el dedo a la garganta y

bueno regurgitate spill not the beans but the wine unholy

there b no blessing in such, as the japoneses se acercan

there be invierten en nuestro ser lo que somos aldea idea

ya caldea ass it were chaldea fell along with babilonia y

sus mil lenguas melcochadas sin quiltas below and above

we remain plucking yerbas pa'que floresca el rosal como

están los rieles en old town bajo el presidio de aquellos que

después de todo erigieron las iglesias arrodillándose pa'ser

flagelados y confundidos con mulas cargando las pieles de

oso curtiendo las de las vacas cortando árboles pa'cer mesas y

ser jusgados infieles para ser crucificados en cárceles sagradas

como ahora las escuelas que no enseñan nada, ni nadar saben

menos hablar con los que producen la riqueza que ellos

gozan filete frances mignón que ufean a todo aquel que no

sea parisino cual, me pregunto es el sino sin calavera que

erija pirámides mexicanas para llevarlas a egipto trazadas en

mate por arquitectos tlamantinimes mayas sin usar ruedas ó

balsas levitando rocas perfectamente labradas y subirlas con

voluntad sin troncos sin esclavos con hartos artesanos sanos

y sabios

Some Chord

some chord feather
drum b some time
sincopated space sin fila tongues
sin cuete tags
vaya pues...camina tu vereda
pa'donde apunte tu hua
mata té ché...solita
...aquí tú está'
con buena chia
una semilla madura que te ayuda'caminal
sin camello
sin caballo
sin elefante, linda indira
mira! mira' tu pie'
que tu' suela' no
tiene neumático' italiano
y te falta pluma'
pa'vola'
culebrea tu'spina dorsal...
...solita la haces...vlin
...tu plexus solar toro, tora
po'l'que de vaca tú no tiene
na'a linda
no abunda...solo permanece
...giorgio first huelga
ATM...atodamadre
august twenty-ninth movimiento
sueños 'bout
laos 'n' cambodia...where..where..u
reserved 2 who...a caballero i hear...
i listen...i pay attention!
me cuadro...con ó sin escuadra

gently
...as it were...   ...simply
   ...sencillo...
            semi auto matic pluma
...how r u?

               i have survived
               smiling without theoretical
post u lates i bear no guns, bear plumas
               luckee 4 us
baby could, would b now gestating
         fidel's puros
                  y plátano macho
   en tostones.....sobre
                     moros y cristianos
pero que digo...eso se llama
            cookeo con ó sin conga
      con cuero y con ganas
            tabaco y ron
      frijoles y ganas mas con maize
...mejor me callo el...¿hocico?..
               soy un animal sapiente
      ...yo no soy ser pien te
das cuenta?...tú...no soy perro
                  jaguar humano
      hermano inperecedero
                  in perece de ero
         ero, el amor mueve
         y facilita ser él, la.
               el que no entiende
   pos allá él los ó las
                  diego rifa con
sus

               rosas y huipiles cantos

'L Amor

'l amor e 'l anarquía
sadness has engulfed
la luna

solar

asphalted ice thrives
heartless blame b cast
weaponless...sin razón
los rios se desbordan while rain
drowns hope, faith prevails
nada mas allá
off 'n' beyond
sand shells shores
with

heart 'n' mind

dogma repertoires aborrecen cualquier luz
off cuff
without singing...sin música
sin amor warrior cantos
bullet words abound coyoteando
corazones rasgados...torn
en la calle fronteriza
no backtracking here tijuana
y tampoco existe vereda

pa'lante

greed 'n' security 'n' fear rule
cats recognize al felino del sur
los gatos escuchan el canto lunar
while flamenco y teponaztles
pluck y tamborilcan
amor y guerra

few realize, muchos se

hacen...

...por no decir

...la mayoría sufre

no se trata de idiosincracia...sin gracia

se trata de carnalismoamor

el trabajo es para todos

so education b Frida

...lest we all starve

...mindless, heart less 'n' bodiless

i'd like 2 sea

the waveful day tabla!

...not yet

...not now

...lots o' work

z do z dice z thrice

z seven...boddhis

know only 4 at best

just keep on sweeping

lighting incense...candles

...off to the cocina

prepare food

...ready the coals 'n' the knives

chop...chop...chop

boil water in a pot

...boil naught the sea!

no beach can b reached that way

silence   b

calpulli rest...tranquilos

...nosotros

...hasta dentro
  entonces somos uno
    da'os cuenta
        ya son mucho mas
    de cien años, mil, dos mil
sesenta mil
        años son los que hemos
           soportadao, doa?
    xicanaie   xicanoia
     ¿...pos ke rifa?
  we have nothing to lose
    but...yours 'n' mine
...our chains must go
    ...the river runs
  stones b hot 'gainst
        the snow...sweat
    pray...
communicate chant...box your way
    out of the underworld
     treasure the gravity grab gnotion
      b one with all
...no dread, locks necessary?
    césare chalice magdalena
the brutality off the streets
    in denver, san juan diego
     or amerindia santa
   feather thy spirit
    sip thy own wine
  blood as it may
    banana chiquita fall

no garfio captain

hook play none

us dolphins

sharks abound...no mahi mahi

no piña

colada from hawaii

cuba sugared puros

corta caña

pa'cer la vida

mas dulce por fa'

entrégate a la vida

this b nut

crack the monopoly game

bring out chips

'n' dance salsa

con chile serrano

ó habanero pero que pique

kill the bull, don't eat the mierda

la cola y los cuernos son tuyos camarada

pain resides

pain resides as deep

as the smile

that adorns the love that crowns it

...césar...napoleón...zapata

could claim this writ

now...

entre dientes

...flossed out

pain b not the opposite of joy

just as much love b not

the opposite of hate

the opposite of love b fear

'n' the opposite of joy

b indifference

...who cares?...for what? love?

...for whom?...whatever was a good

a very good

...pluma!!!

wasn't even

a monk then...

inkless!!! lead was 'n' continues

to b a weapon

wooded...

encased

...deadly...sharper than any

swordtongue or bulletmind, i lápiz!

bullying any one

of us simple mayamexican

duendes gitano amorosos

¿a ver...quien nos

saca el corazón...?

one of these theys

i shall go to yougo es labia

'n' forget my family not

in bosnia

pluck no strings

'n' forget india 'n' sevilla

uno de estos dias

i shall deny my

heritage...?

...not today!...hokay!!!

maya...vasco...moro...gitano

the garlic 'n' the sage b ours

the candle

b

gitana

hermana

...what do u know...no nothing?

wallow...paloma...the tanks

the asphalt

...b just a kiss...a la vuelta

a corazón

a'spiri tú

alto

leche...café...chocolate...canela

pinole...atole

así, we won't feed the people

clothe the people

house the people

así la educación...not suficiente

no será para todos

...¿sabes, ke nó???

Vixens

Vixens are stalking in quiet treacherous ways. The hunted within gather forces. Men, white as ever, think their little bitches can scarf on our ocelot flesh, bones and blood. Assured be that we, felines, will continue to roar in spite of all gangs that hunt us. The Earthmother will tremble as we recover our forests and Tlaloquitos shall clear our air wetly. Milpas shall prevail and so will all our relatives. In the labyrinths of this neofascist burrocracia, nosotros, those who chose to enter the halls and institutions that have been founded "for all," have confronted the ice in "just us" which we clearly are naught. We refuse to bark at their waning moon, at the cartilage of fish thrown as trash for us to survive on. Equal opportunity to die now or pay taxes without the education that schooling has yet to provide; success?...Kiss Ass 101...Course Description still to be written.

Dr. George Pleonasm hath his slaves develop the course in chains and big lips on his ass. Georgie savored the tattoo; some slaves had inked teeth.

COURSE DESCRIPTION

We shall examine our chains and lick them. The wisdom of the master shall not be questioned. The mistress shall be honored and adored regardless of her ugliness, ignorance and klutsiness. If female thou shall spread your legs; if male thou shall bend over and take as many lashes as the mistress requires for your indifferent cock. You all shall rise at the crack of dawn and genuflect to cotton though you be naked. If Mexican though, remember the holiest words: "Si siñour." Bear your hat in your hands, and stare at the ground...dare not look into your master's eyes.

COURSE OBJECTIVES

I.   Produce the master's wealth so that he may enjoy it.

II.   Serve with a smile as your master farts and frolics your life and spirit away.

III. Perform all master's dirty work including hatchetmen duty in spite of your brothers and sisters.

IV.   Disguise the master's work as your sinful undoing. Bear his cross after you have made the nails and carved the wood. Rejoice.

V.   Bless your master's life unto the heaven you have created for him as you descend unto the hell he has doomed and slaved you with on earth with his greed.

Meditation Canto

give yourself 2 the creative intelligence that
rules our destiny. hold on 2 nothing, treasure
your heart.
hold on 2 no description of what is in order
2 see the great architect's design.
let go of fear in order 2 experience love 'n'
remember that we matter, that we count.
serene 'n' detached, embrace the will of
the universe, cosmic love 'n' spiritual
freedom from all self-destructive thoughts,
all enslaving routines, 'n' all loveless
relationships.
b one with the creator 'n' flow with
peaceful energy 'n' joy. yes. love.
b we.

alurista
Aztlán 2010